BEYOND
THE THEORY:
SCIENCE
OF THE FUTURE

ARE WE ALONE IN THE UNIVERSE?

THEORIES ABOUT INTELLIGENT LIFE ON OTHER PLANETS

Tom Jackson

Gareth Stevens
PUBLISHING

Please visit our website, www.garethstevens.com.
For a free color catalog of all our high-quality books,
call toll free 1-800-542-2595 or fax 1-877-542-2596.

Cataloging-in-Publication Data

Names: Jackson, Tom.
Title: Are we alone in the universe? theories about intelligent life on other planets / Tom Jackson.
Description: New York : Gareth Stevens Publishing, 2019. | Series: Beyond the theory: science of the future |
Includes glossary and index.
Identifiers: LCCN ISBN 9781538226742 (pbk.) | ISBN 9781538226735 (library bound)
Subjects: LCSH: Life on other planets--Juvenile literature. | Life (Biology)--Juvenile literature. | Extrasolar
planets--Juvenile literature.
Classification: LCC QB54.J33 2019 | DDC 576.8'39--dc23

First Edition

Published in 2019 by
Gareth Stevens Publishing
111 East 14th Street, Suite 349
New York, NY 10003

© 2019 Gareth Stevens Publishing

Produced for Gareth Stevens by Calcium
Editors: Sarah Eason and Tim Cooke
Designers: Emma DeBanks and Lynne Lennon
Picture researcher: Rachel Blount

Picture credits: Cover: Shutterstock: Andrii Vodolazhskyi; Inside: NASA: p. 33; NASA Goddard Space Flight
Center Image by Reto Stöckli: p. 8; NASA/JPL: pp. 17, 30; NASA/JPL-Caltech: p. 43; NASA/JPLCaltech/MSSS:
p. 32; Shutterstock: Edwin Butter: p. 10; Siriwatthana Chankawee: p. 21b; CrackerClips Stock Media: p. 39;
Andrea Crisante: p. 24; Evenfh: p. 21t; John Foreman: p. 29; Foto-Ruhrgebiet: p. 12; Ggw: p. 27; Bird Haven:
p. 5b; Kobimanop: p. 9; Lotus_studio: p. 4; Karsten Neglia: p. 7; Nobeastsofierce: p. 6; Antonio Jorge Nunes:
p. 5t; Ana Aguirre Perez: pp. 1, 25; Ranjith Ravindran: p. 11; Supadech Sanguannam: p. 26; Sdecoret: p. 38; J.R.
Skok: p. 31b; Gary Yim: p. 18; Michal Zduniak: p. 13; Wikimedia Commons: pp. 19, 34; ESO/L. Calçada: p. 37;
ESO/DSS 2: p. 42; G.Gillet/ESO: p. 36; NASA: pp. 15t, 23, 31t; NASA Ames/ W Stenzel: p. 16; NASA Goddard
Space Flight Center: p. 28; NASA/JPL: pp. 14, 15b; NASA/JPL-Caltech: p. 41; Arne Nordmann (norro): p. 35;
Giovanni Schiaparelli: p. 22; Vedexent: p. 40; Bartolomeu Velho: p. 20.

Printed in the United States of America

CPSIA compliance information: Batch #CS18GS:
For further information contact Gareth Stevens, New York, New York at 1-800-542-2595.

CONTENTS

CHAPTER 1

LIFE-FORMS

Earth is home to 8 million **species** of life—at least. The true number may be 10 times that. Life occurs in so many places on Earth that scientists have trouble counting all the species. If there are so many species on Earth, what is the chance that there is at least one more species that lives in another part of the universe?

Life on Earth is dominated by one species—us. Humans use technology to create our own living conditions and alter nature to meet our needs. In other words we have a **civilization**, something no other animal has.

Coral reefs support a wide diversity of weird and wonderful life-forms.

Rainforests are some of the most diverse habitats on Earth, with species from tiny insects to large mammals.

Human civilization has even managed to go beyond Earth into space—although so far we have not gone very far. The only permanent human settlement in space, the International Space Station, is about 250 miles (400 km) above Earth. That is 50 times higher than Mount Everest—but still only a fraction of the distance to another **planet**.

Space scientists are planning for humans to travel farther into space. The first destinations would be the moon and Mars. Where better to start searching for **aliens** than our own space neighborhood? And if we find them, what will that say about alien life on other planets orbiting distant stars? If there are aliens in other **solar systems**, what are the chances that they are intelligent enough to be space travelers like us? And will we ever be able to make contact with them across the vast distances of space? To find out, we need to go beyond the theory.

The moon is one of the first places scientists have looked for alien life.

BEING ALIVE

Humans have a head start in the search for aliens. Even before we have any evidence they exist, we already know a very important fact about them. They are alive.

Being alive is very complex. Earth has many varieties of life that survive using different techniques. However, despite all the complexity, **biologists** have found that all life on Earth is defined by a simple set of tasks. Alien life will have to do the same tasks, too. However, it may achieve them in weird ways.

Any definition of life has to include simple life-forms such as **bacteria**.

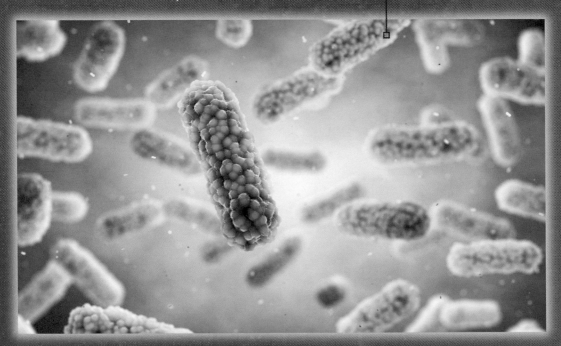

UNANSWERED

Some objects do some but not all of MERRING. For example, a car moves and is "fed" with gasoline. It respires this fuel to release energy, excreting the exhaust gases. The latest autopilot systems also make the car aware of its surroundings. However, a car cannot grow or reproduce—yet! Aliens, if they exist, will have to do all of MERRING—and that will help us find them.

Driverless cars display many qualities of living things— yet they are clearly not alive.

The basic requirements of life are summed up with a memory aid: MERRING. M stands for movement, E is for excretion, R is for respiration, the second R is for reproduction, I is for irritability, N is for nutrition, and the G is for growth. Most of these are obvious, apart from irritability. The acronym MERRING needed a second vowel (otherwise it wouldn't be pronounceable), so "irritability" was used instead of the more obvious "senses." They both mean that all life is able to detect the changes in its environment and respond to them.

All animals move at some point in their lives. Plants move, too, but far more slowly, usually toward light. Excretion is the removal of waste materials from inside the body. Respiration is using chemical reactions to extract energy from food. Reproduction refers to life's ability to create new versions of itself. All life needs a source of energy, which is summed up as nutrition. Finally, all living things grow, either by getting steadily bigger or by dividing to create more bodies.

EVIDENCE OF LIFE

From space, Earth appears as a marvelous "blue marble" with white clouds and patches of green. However, by itself its appearance does not show that there is life down here. Like Earth, any planet with life as we know it will display three giveaway clues: liquid water, pure oxygen, and complex carbon molecules. All three are essential for life as we define it.

The sequence of chemical reactions that takes place inside all living things is called metabolism. All metabolism takes place in water, because the chemicals involved float around in water. Life on Earth probably began in the oceans and only later moved to dry land. In order to survive on land, life-forms developed ways to hold water inside their bodies. Water is also involved in a very important part of **biochemistry**. Life needs a supply of energy, all of which comes from the sun. A plant's leaves collect the energy in sunlight and then use the energy to combine water with carbon dioxide to make sugar, the simplest form of food.

The first color photograph of Earth taken from space in 1972 was dubbed the "Blue Marble."

UNANSWERED

It may be possible that alien life is based on silicon molecules instead of carbon. However, because silicon atoms bond together weakly, these life-forms would not survive for long. On Earth, some bacteria do not use sunlight as a source of energy. They harvest energy from rocks, mainly as the gas hydrogen sulfide. Alien life might do something similar. However, instead of giving out oxygen, these organisms are left with solid sulfur in their bodies. Again, it is hard to imagine how sulfurous life-forms could develop into more complex—and intelligent—life-forms.

That process is called photosynthesis. It releases pure oxygen as a waste product. The oxygen ends up in Earth's **atmosphere** and is a signal that life is using energy to convert simple raw materials into more complex and useful chemicals. Life-forms then use the oxygen to reverse the process, through a chemical reaction called respiration. The oxygen consumed by life-forms "burns" the food they consume in order to release stored energy for life to use.

The energy is used to build yet more complicated chemicals, which build up the living body. These chemicals are all based on complex clusters of carbon atoms, with other chemicals attached. Only carbon can form the chains, rings, and networks required to build living tissue. You cannot build living bodies from any other element. So wherever we see liquid water, pure oxygen, and complex carbon, we will find life.

Leaves convert the energy in sunlight into sugar that provides food for trees.

DO ALIENS
HAVE GENES?

Life on Earth is based on complex chainlike molecules called nucleic acids. The main nucleic acids are deoxyribonucleic acid (DNA) and ribonucleic acid (RNA). These are the chemicals that carry genes, which are the instructions for making a living body. Genes would be a key aspect of any alien life.

Genes pass the instructions for life from parents to their offspring.

Once genetic chemicals appeared on Earth, the simple forms of early life became more complex. Bacteria and mold developed into plants, animals, and intelligent beings like us. Scientists understand the process quite well. However, understanding just how genetic systems appeared in the first place will be a key aspect to finding aliens.

Earth's genetic system is thought to have developed from the ability of a few chemicals, including RNA, to make copies of themselves. RNA's long molecule acts as a template for smaller sections to line up and bond together. RNA (and DNA) molecules have different units chained together in many different orders. Some versions of RNA began to team up with other molecules that helped them replicate, or copy, themselves, such as proteins. These molecules formed protective coatings or helped make replication faster.

UNANSWERED

DNA carries its genetic code as a set of four chemical units, which are put together in a specific order, like the letters in a sentence. The units are more or less the same size, so jumbling their order does not change the overall shape and strength of the DNA molecule. Alien life could work in the same way (although it will probably use different "letters"). Alien hunters attach chemical detectors to space **probes** to sniff out any alien chemicals that work like our DNA.

The precise structure of each RNA chain became a code for making these helper chemicals—and the codes became the first genes. DNA is like a doubled-up version of RNA, so it can protect its codes even better. By growing longer and adding more genes, the most successful versions of these complex chemicals built bags around themselves, where they could store raw materials. In other words, they became the first **cells**—the first living bodies. The rest is history. (In fact, it is natural history!)

If alien life exists, it will use chemicals like DNA. However, these substances are too complex to form by themselves. Where did they come from? There are two possible options: mud and space!

DNA is structured as a double helix: a pair of chains connected with rungs, like a spiraling ladder.

WHERE DID LIFE START?

Earth's fossils tell us a lot about how life has changed over billions of years. A fossil is evidence of a long-dead life-form that has turned into rock. A fossil might be of a body part such as bones, a footprint, or an empty space left by a body that has decayed. Fossils reveal that life started as simple bacteria-like organisms about 4 billion years ago. If it started that way here, it has probably started on other planets, too.

Ammonites are sea creatures that lived over 65 million years ago.

There are two very different theories about where life on Earth started. The first suggests that life developed from mud, while the second says it came from space. Most scientists support the first theory, which is sometimes called the Primordial Soup. This theory suggests that RNA (and later DNA) developed by chance in a **reactive** chemical soup. This soup existed in the warm mud around hydrothermal vents. These are volcanic springs on the seabed that pump out boiling hot water. The early Earth was a violent place, with asteroid strikes and volcanic eruptions. Today, the deep sea is an extreme habitat. Back then, however, the seabed around the boiling vents was probably the most stable place to live. Alien hunters look for other worlds that also have hydrothermal vents, which could act as nurseries to create life.

BEHIND THE THEORY

In 1952, Stanley Miller, a young American chemist, tried to re-create the Primordial Soup. He mixed the chemicals present on the early Earth before life appeared. Miller then ran his "soup" through an apparatus that boiled it, stirred it, electrified it, and cooled it, as would have happened in Earth's ancient seas and air. After a day, the mixture went pink. After a week, it contained many chemicals usually associated with life. This suggested that if the experiment ran for millions of years, it would eventually produce many more complex chemicals— and then perhaps RNA and DNA...

The second idea of how life began is called panspermia. It suggests that life arrived on Earth inside a **meteorite**, a rock from space mixed with ice and dust. Nucleic acids or even bacteria could have been frozen deep inside these "dirty snowballs." However, meteorites that hit Earth today do not contain any lifelike chemicals. In addition, if meteorites did contain such chemicals, where did they originate? The panspermia theory does not really answer the key question: Where did life start?

A meteorite may have carried simple forms of life to Earth.

CHAPTER 2

A PLACE TO LIVE

The most likely place to find aliens is on a planet like Earth. Our planet is in the habitable zone of the solar system. It is close enough to the sun for its surface to be warmed to a temperature where water is a liquid, but not so close that the sun's heat boils the water away. Any farther from the sun, and the lack of heat would make the planet freeze into a giant snowball.

Earth's position in the solar system is also known as the Goldilocks' Orbit. Like Goldilocks trying the porridge of the three bears, it is "not too hot, and not too cold—just right." The average temperature of Earth is about 60.8°F (16°C), although it varies widely. This kind of temperature is ideal for the chemical reactions used by life. For example, above about 140°F (60°C), metabolism starts going wrong as proteins begin to break apart.

As the third planet from the sun, Earth is ideally positioned in the solar system to support life.

The surface of Mars resembles that of some deserts on Earth.

Because we assume that aliens need liquid water and use a carbon-based chemistry like us, we need to look for alien life in the sun's habitable zone. However, calculating the size of this zone is not easy. The surface temperature of Earth is warmed by the **greenhouse effect**, in which the atmosphere traps heat. Without this warming, Earth's oceans would be mostly frozen over.

Some astronomers think that the habitable zone of the solar system includes the planets Venus and Mars and some larger asteroids. Maybe primitive life-forms exist in these places, or perhaps they did long ago. In addition, space probes have found liquid water beneath the surface of moons orbiting Jupiter and Saturn. These are several times farther from the sun than Earth, but might they be included in the habitable zone as well?

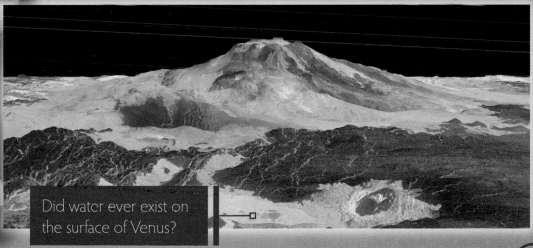

Did water ever exist on the surface of Venus?

EXOPLANETS

Until 20 years ago, no one knew if our solar system was unique. It was impossible to see other stars clearly enough to tell if they were orbited by their own planets. Then, in 1992, astronomers discovered the first exoplanet—a planet orbiting another star. Since then, they have found thousands more. Are they looking at the homes of alien civilizations?

Astronomers find exoplanets using two main techniques. The first is to look to find a star that regularly dims slightly. This might mean a planet is moving between the star and Earth. The *Kepler* spacecraft, which orbits the sun, uses this method to identify stars likely to have exoplanets.

The *Kepler* spacecraft is looking for Earth-sized planets orbiting other stars.

Telescopes on Earth then check these stars by looking for tiny wobbles in their motion. Planets are held in orbit by their star's **gravity**, but in return the planet's gravity gives the star a little tug, creating a giveaway wobble. The size of the wobble shows how big the planet is.

The *Kepler* mission has revealed that nearly all stars have at least two planets. Most stars have several, like our own sun. There are 200 billion stars in our **galaxy** alone. That would mean there are perhaps a trillion (1,000 billion) exoplanets out there in our galaxy, the **Milky Way**. If the chances of a planet having intelligent life are just one in a billion—that's very low—then the Milky Way could still have 1,000 civilizations. The Milky Way is just one of billions of galaxies in the universe. Do the math: the numbers of exoplanets are mind-boggling.

This poster celebrates the discovery of the first exoplanet, 51 Pegasi b.

UNANSWERED

Exoplanets like Earth will be rocky worlds in the habitable zone of stars. The size, weight, and position of an exoplanet tells us what it might be made of, and the size of its star tells us how hot the planet is. Most exoplanets orbit red dwarf stars, which are smaller and cooler than our sun. So far most exoplanets are called Hot Jupiters. They are huge balls of gas orbiting close to their suns. Others are Mini-Neptunes, which are small lumps of ice orbiting farther out. Rocky planets like Earth are much smaller and harder to spot, but the search continues.

ASTROBIOLOGY

There is a scientific name for alien hunting: astrobiology. It means roughly "star life science." Astrobiologists' job is to find alien life. They start by figuring out where to look for life. Then they try to imagine what kinds of things they are looking for—so they will recognize it when they find it.

Astrobiologists start by understanding life on Earth. They look at the many ways life-forms are able to survive in different and extreme habitats, from the deep seas to the driest deserts. Next, they look for these habitats on other worlds. If they find them, the astrobiologists ask themselves how aliens would survive there and what they would look like. They take into account how conditions on other planets are likely to differ from conditions on Earth, such as the pull of gravity, the pressure of the atmosphere, and the length of the days and nights.

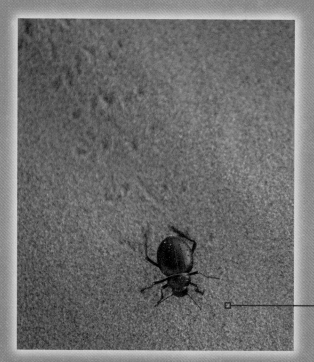

So far astrobiologists have not found another planet like Earth, although they have identified a few exoplanets that might turn out to be similar to our own. Nevertheless, an astrobiologist could not visit such a world or even send a robotic probe to investigate. It would take centuries (at least) to fly there.

Astrobiologists study how animals on Earth cope with extreme conditions.

BEHIND THE THEORY

The first astrobiologist was the Russian astronomer Gavriil Adrianovich Tikhov. He got the idea from his countryman, Konstantin Tsiolkovsky. Tsiolkovsky was the world's first rocket engineer. In 1903, he showed it should be possible to travel into space. Tsiolkovsky suggested that humans could set up farms in space or on other planets. Tikhov came up with the idea for astrobiology as he was searching for places where plants could grow in space.

Gavriil Tikhov (right) searches for locations in space that might support life.

Instead, astrobiologists concentrate on finding life in our own part of space. Probes to Mars are looking for signs of life, and there are plans to send probes to Enceladus and Europa, two ice moons with oceans under their surface. Venus and the asteroid Ceres are also candidates for an astrobiology mission.

If an astrobiologist ever finds an alien, then that will put an end to the science. In its place a new kind of researcher will appear: an exobiologist. That term means something like "alien life scientist."

INVENTING ALIENS

Until the sixteenth century, most people believed that Earth was at the center of the universe. The moon and sun moved around Earth, together with the five planets then known. The stars were lights hanging on the inside of a vast sphere that formed the edge of the heavens. Then in 1543, the Polish astronomer Nicolaus Copernicus shook the world by showing that Earth was just the third planet in our sun's solar system.

This map of the universe, drawn in 1568, ignores Copernicus's theory and places Earth at the center.

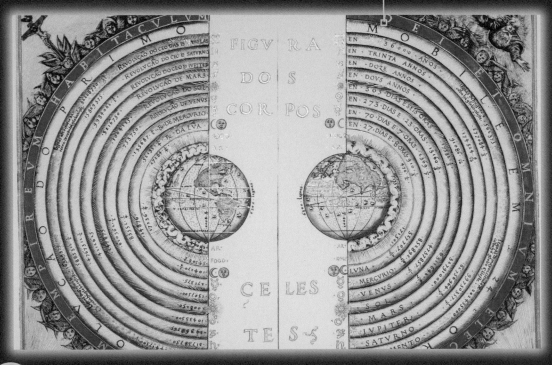

Are Easter Island's famous statues depictions of visitors from outer space?

Today, we know that the universe is very big, with an unimaginable number of galaxies, stars, and planets. Even before people learned this, however, they started to wonder if there were other worlds around other stars. If there were, it stood to reason that beings like us might live there, too. The idea of aliens was born. While astronomers searched the heavens for them, other people wondered if aliens had already visited Earth. Perhaps ancient stories of gods were really about aliens.

One example people used was the Nazca Lines. About 2,500 years ago, the Nazca people of Peru started scraping designs in the desert. They include animals and figures that look like people in spacesuits. The shapes are so large that they can only be seen from overhead. The site includes straight lines and rectangles some people think were guides and landing strips for alien craft. There are many other more believable explanations for the Nazca Lines and other mysterious ancient sites. But people still love stories about aliens. Just remember they are only stories—probably!

The Nazca Lines in the desert of Peru include this huge spider.

LOOKING FOR MARTIANS

In the early days of scientific astronomy, astronomers believed humans were not alone in the solar system. A mistranslation on a map of Mars created the biggest alien hunt in history. It led to many significant discoveries.

In 1877, the Italian astronomer Giovanni Schiaparelli drew a map of Mars showing many canyons, which he labeled *canali*, which means "channels" in Italian. When his map was printed in English, however, *canali* was translated into "canal"—meaning artificial river. For many people, this confirmed what they already thought. Aliens on Mars would have to be very organized to survive.

Schiaparelli's map of Mars appeared to show artificial canals.

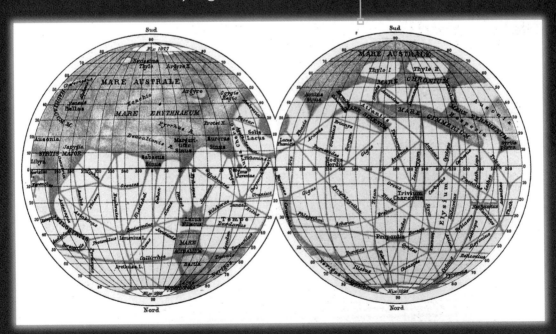

Constance Lowell began interfering in his **observatory**. She argued with Vesto Slipher over money. When Pluto was discovered, Constance insisted it be named Percival. Clyde Tombaugh wanted to call it Diana, after the goddess of hunting. In the end the name was decided by a competition, which was won by an 11-year-old girl from England.

Vesto Slipher learned that galaxies were moving away from Earth.

In 1894, Percival Lowell, a US businessman, built an observatory near Flagstaff, Arizona, to look for more evidence of the Martians. He did not find any. After his retirement, Vesto Slipher used the observatory to study "spiral nebulae"—fuzzy cloud shapes among the stars. He found they were all moving away from Earth. The spiral nebulae were later renamed galaxies, and Slipher's information helped to show that the universe was constantly expanding in all directions. In 1930, one of Slipher's helpers, Clyde Tombaugh, found Planet X, which is now known as the dwarf planet Pluto.

UFOS

Every year, people report seeing several thousand unidentified flying objects, or UFOs. Although UFOs are much more common now, people have been recording strange objects flying in the sky for thousands of years. Some people believe that UFOs are alien spacecraft visiting Earth, but this has never been proven—so far.

The first ever UFO was recorded in 1400 BC in ancient Egypt. Glowing disks appeared in the sky during the day. There were similar reports through history, but the number of sightings began to increase in the nineteenth century. In the last 100 years, there have been more than 100,000 reported sightings of UFOs, and the number increases every year. (You are 300 times more likely to spot UFOs if you live in the United States than anywhere else in the world.)

Is the increase because aliens have started visiting Earth more regularly (especially North America)? Or does it reflect the growth in **science fiction** about aliens, such as *War of the Worlds*, *Superman*, and *Flash Gordon*?

Flying saucers are a particularly common form of UFO.

BEHIND THE THEORY

J. Allen Hynek , a leading UFO expert, created a system for classifying UFOs. A close encounter of the first kind is when someone gets a clear view of a UFO. The second kind is when a UFO has some effect on the observer or their surroundings, such as lights going out or scorching the ground. A close encounter of the third kind is when the occupants of the UFO make contact with the human observer.

The growth of reports of UFOs also coincided with the age of air travel New flying machines— balloons, airships, rockets, helicopters, and airplanes—were appearing for the first time. They may have influenced people's reports.

People often describe UFOs as "flying saucers"—round machines that hover and swoop at great speeds. This idea became common in the 1930s, around the time Henri Coanda, a Romanian aviator, invented a real-life flying saucer. It did not work very well, but we now know that top-secret aircraft were developed in the twentieth century. Were these the real UFOs?

Some artists imagine UFOs as hollow spheres.

ARE WE ACTUALLY ALONE?

Every day there seems to be bad news from somewhere in the world. There are also many worries for the future, such as climate change, war, environmental destruction, and disease. However, we should never forget the fact that human civilization is a remarkable phenomenon. Humans have achieved many amazing things—and will continue to do so. Despite what people sometimes think, by most standards, civilization is getting better all the time. Human beings are very special indeed.

Earth's home galaxy, the Milky Way, is visible on clear nights as a long cloud of light.

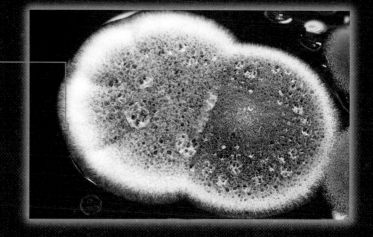

Alien life is more likely to resemble bacteria than complex creatures like humans.

The question is just how special are we? In the 1960s, the American astronomer Frank Drake used mathematics to calculate the chance that other civilizations existed. Drake's math is now called the Drake **Equation**. The equation included the rate at which stars formed, the proportion of stars that had planets, and the proportion of those planets that were in the habitable zone.

The equation takes such factors into account to calculate the likelihood of alien life existing. Although some of the numbers used in the Drake Equation are only informed guesswork, the chances look very high that life does indeed exist elsewhere. All the information we have about the universe suggests that there are many, many places where the conditions for life exist. We don't know exactly where yet. It may be elsewhere in the solar system, but life is almost certain to be out there in our galaxy and beyond.

However, astrobiologists are looking for any kind of life—not just life that resembles humans. If they find life, it will probably be green goo rather than green men. Most alien planets are more likely to be home to simple bacteria-like organisms than intelligent, civilized beings. The Drake Equation includes numbers to figure out the chances of alien life being intelligent and having communications technology, such as **radio** signals, that would allow us to detect them—and perhaps make contact. These numbers are harder to estimate than the likelihood of life existing. The chances of intelligent life may be tiny. Earth might be the only planet where there is life capable of understanding its place in the universe. It may be that there is plenty of alien life—but none we can talk to.

RARE EARTH

To figure out the chances of intelligent life developing on other planets, astrobiologists looked at what it is about Earth and its place in space that helped it become a civilized world. What they found suggests that our planet is very rare indeed.

The solar system is far from the center of the galaxy. That means it is protected from shockwaves from exploding giant stars and bursts of energy from **black holes** at the heart of the Milky Way. However, Earth is not right out on the edge of the galaxy, where there are too few of the chemicals needed to make rock. The sun is a small, slow-burning star. That gave the planet enough time—about 4 billion years—for simple life to develop into humans. Bigger, brighter stars would burn out before life had a chance to evolve. However, the sun is also big enough to possess a large habitable zone. The habitable zones of smaller stars are so small that planets are locked by the star's gravity.

Winds from the sun blast away atmospheres from planets without a magnetic core.

At one-sixth the size of Earth, our moon is huge compared to the size of the moons of other planets.

One side of the planet always faces the star and is very hot, while the other side faces away and is very cold. There is no cycle of day and night to even out such planets' surface temperatures. Earth is also well protected. The gravity of Jupiter, our huge neighbor, pulls away most meteorites that might crash into us. The planet's metallic core creates a magnetic field that prevents the electrified **solar wind** from blasting away the atmosphere.

So Earth has a civilization because it is in the right part of the galaxy, in the right part of the solar system, orbiting the right kind of star, with the right kind of neighbors, and the right kind of atmosphere and rocks—and the right kind of moon. What are the chances?

UNANSWERED

The leading theory on the creation of the moon— called the Big Splash—says that a Mars-sized planet smashed into the young Earth. The two planets merged, flinging chunks of rock into orbit that joined together to make the moon. The impact tilted Earth's axis, which now creates seasons—another feature that reduces extreme surface conditions. The Big Splash also thinned the atmosphere, reducing the greenhouse effect, and cooling Earth to just the right temperature.

CHAPTER 5

THE SEARCH FOR ALIENS

People have been looking for signs of alien life for the last 100 years. The development of space technology is allowing us to explore the solar system. So far scientists have not found definite proof of alien life— but the search continues.

In the 1960s, humans sent the first probes to fly past our neighboring planets, Venus and Mars. The probes took close-up photos and measured the chemicals in the planets' atmospheres. The air on both Venus and Mars contained gases associated with life, such as methane and carbon dioxide.

The next phase was to send landers to explore the surface of other planets. Venus's atmosphere was so thick that lightweight space probes were squashed before they reached the ground. Tougher probes later landed, but Venus was so hot—840°F (450°C)—that the instruments melted. (The planet's **acid rain** did not help either.) Astrobiologists think super-tough life-forms could live in Venus's rocks—as they do on Earth—but there are no plans to go and check.

This photograph of Venus was taken by the *Magellan* probe launched in 1989.

These tiny cell-like objects may be evidence of ancient life on Mars.

Instead, most alien-hunting missions go to Mars. The first was the Viking program, which placed two landers on Mars in the 1970s. The landers sent back details of the chemistry of Martian rocks. Today Mars rovers are continuing the search for aliens—but the best evidence of Martian life has come from a rock found on Earth.

In 1984, scientists identified a meteorite in Antarctica as a piece of Martian rock that had been flung into space by another meteor impact 17 million years ago, eventually hitting Earth after spending millennia in space. In 1996, scientists found tiny cell-like objects in the rock, which is known as ALH84001. No one is sure, but it is possible that these are the remains of ancient alien life that once lived on Mars—before the planet dried out and became the cold desert we know today.

ALH84001 fell to Earth as a meteorite in Antarctica around 13,000 years ago.

ROBOT EXPLORERS

Several nations have declared ambitions to send humans to Mars by the middle of the twenty-first century. The voyage will be long, dangerous, and expensive. If Mars has a supply of water, the mission would be much easier. The water could be used for drinking and be converted into rocket fuel for the flight home. It could even make it possible to set up farms to support a future space **colony**. So the search is on for water—and where there is water, there could be alien life, too.

The *Curiosity* rover has been exploring the surface of Mars since 2012.

In 2003, the National Aeronautics and Space Administration (NASA) landed two robotic rovers on Mars named *Spirit* and *Opportunity*. The rovers had 3D cameras so controllers on Earth could steer them better. They also had scoops for scraping up dust and instruments to analyze its contents. Powered with **solar panels**, the rovers shut down in the Martian winter and started up again when the weather got brighter.

UNANSWERED

Europa, Jupiter's fourth moon, has a thick sheet of ice covering an ocean of water. Heated water sometimes breaks through the ice as geysers. This shows there is a source of heat inside the moon—and maybe aliens, too. The *Europa Clipper* is due to land on the moon in the 2020s to collect water samples. Scientists have to make sure not to contaminate Europa with bacteria from Earth. Otherwise we could make all the aliens sick—and kill them just as we discover them!

Spirit lasted more than seven years, and *Opportunity* was still going 15 years after landing. Neither rover found water, although the way the Martian dust was layered suggested that the planet was once covered in oceans and rivers.

In 2008, the *Phoenix* lander had more luck. Using a shovel to dig holes into the surface, it found that Mars had small amounts of water ice beneath its surface. Next up was *Curiosity*, which arrived in 2012. It has a **radioactive** engine, so it never has to stop working. *Curiosity* is equipped with a drill to get deep into rocks. If life exists on Mars—or existed in the past—this is where the evidence will be. NASA believes it will find these alien **microbes** within 10 years.

Europa's buried ocean may contain three times as much water as Earth's oceans!

HELLO, EARTH CALLING

It is not possible to send probes to exoplanets beyond our solar system. Alien hunters are therefore forced to use a different technique. They are listening to the universe!

In 1936, a powerful TV signal was used to broadcast the opening ceremony of the Olympic Games in Berlin, Germany, around the world. The signal used radio waves, and was the first signal strong enough to leak out into space. It has been traveling away from Earth at the speed of light ever since. The radio waves have been spreading out and getting weaker as they go, but an advanced alien civilization could turn them into pictures. If so, their first view of an Earthling might be Germany's dictator in 1936—Adolf Hitler!

Radio signals from the 1936 Berlin Olympics are still traveling across the universe!

BEHIND THE THEORY

In the 1980s, two probes, *Voyager 1* and *2*, explored Jupiter, Saturn, and the outer planets. When the mission ended, the *Voyagers* headed out of the solar system. US scientist Carl Sagan realized that the probes might be found by aliens. He convinced NASA to include some information about our planet on the probes, on gramophone records made from aluminum coated with gold. Each record holds music, voices, and pictures from Earth—plus some instructions on how to make a record player!

The Arecibo Message of 1974 was a coded picture.

In the 1930s, researchers discovered that stars give out radio waves as well as light. In the 1980s, the Search for Extraterrestrial Intelligence (SETI) began scanning the jumble of radio waves from space. It looked for deliberate signals sent by intelligent beings. Nothing has been found. Scientists have used focused beams of radio waves to send messages from Earth to nearby stars in our galaxy. They include the Arecibo Message of 1974, written by the American scientists Frank Drake and Carl Sagan. In 2008, the Doritos company beamed an advertisement for tortilla chips to a planet in the Big Dipper! If aliens do want some chips, their reply should reach us in 2094.

AN EXTREMELY
LARGE TELESCOPE

Instead of waiting to hear from alien civilizations, astronomers are eager to start looking for them. However, other planets are so far away that our telescopes cannot really see them. In order to solve this problem, astronomers are building a very big telescope indeed.

The telescope is being assembled at the European Southern Observatory (ESO) in the high, dry deserts of Chile. When finished in 2024, the instrument will be called the Extremely Large Telescope (ELT). It will be the largest telescope ever built. Its main mirror is 129 feet (39.3 m) wide—it would cover a third of a football field. This mirror bounces light from space around three more mirrors before the light is focused into a camera.

The European Space Observatory already has a Very Large Telescope (VLT).

BEHIND THE THEORY

The British scientist James Lovelock is most famous for the Gaia **Hypothesis**. This is a way of understanding planet Earth as a single living system. Lovelock had the idea while working on the Viking program for NASA, thinking up ways of finding aliens on Mars. He realized that the amounts of gases in Earth's atmosphere are constantly changing. These changes are due to life on the planet. Any other living planet must have this same kind of changing atmosphere—so that is what the ELT will look for.

The ELT's fourth mirror can change shape as starlight twinkles, warping and rippling 1,000 times a second to cancel out any fuzziness. Combined with smart controls, this means the ELT will be able to see about 15 times better than the Hubble Space Telescope, which is in orbit above Earth.

As well as studying baby stars as they develop, the ELT's main goal is to look for exoplanets, including small, rocky ones like Earth. The colors of light it collects from the planets' atmospheres will reveal what gases are present there—and that will be the best chance of finding other Earths, teeming with life.

This is an artist's concept of the completed ELT.

CHAPTER 6

FIRST CONTACT

What will happen when we meet aliens for the first time? Scientists call that event first contact. First contact will obviously be a very significant moment in Earth's history. That is, if it has not already happened—in secret.

The idea of first contact originally came from science-fiction stories. However, serious scientists are now thinking about what to do if we do ever meet aliens. In stories, the contact generally occurs when an alien from a super-advanced civilization comes to Earth. If first contact ever does happen, however, it is possible it will be the other way around. Humans might be the advanced civilization, and the aliens might be bugs and critters that do not even realize that contact has been made!

Scientists are figuring out plans to deal with first contact with alien visitors.

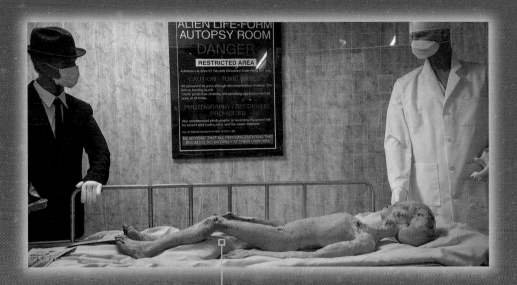

The **autopsy** on an alien from Roswell, New Mexico, was later revealed as a **hoax**.

Examples from human history suggest that civilizations are prone to conflicts and wars. Would aliens try to colonize Earth, as Europe colonized the Americas? Or would humans be the first to attack? We will also have to take precautions so we do not catch diseases from the aliens—nor they from us. If something goes wrong—say, if people start getting sick—will humans simply try to destroy the aliens in order to protect themselves and Earth?

Some people think humans have already made first contact with alien travelers. A leading contender for this is the Roswell Incident of 1947. An unknown craft crashed outside the New Mexico town of Roswell, and the area was sealed off by the military. Rumors persisted for years that aliens had landed and were being kept secret by the government. In the 1990s, a video of an alien autopsy appeared. It was later revealed as a hoax. The US Air Force eventually admitted it had been testing a device for detecting atomic explosions using a high-altitude balloon that crashed. All the secrecy had been in order to prevent anyone finding out about this vital technology.

In the Roswell story, humans were in control of the aliens' arrival. If we are ever visited by advanced aliens for real, however, it will not be humans who are in control. Let's hope any visitors are friendly!

BUSINESS, PLEASURE, OR INVASION?

Imagine an alien civilization that had the technology to travel great distances between solar systems. Would they come? What would they want? Perhaps it would be better not to find out.

Civilizations might surround their star with a sphere of solar panels.

Our own civilization is many decades, and probably centuries, from being able to fly to other stars. If we decide that making contact with other civilizations is not too dangerous, where would we decide to look?

Any civilization needs energy to power its technology. Some scientists predict that advanced alien civilizations would have to surround their suns with immense arrays of solar panels to get energy or even build vast living spaces around suns. Such structures are named Dyson Spheres for Freeman Dyson, the American mathematician who thought them up. A Dyson Sphere would absorb some of the star's light, making it grow suddenly dim. A dimming star might therefore be a sign of an alien civilization. In 2015, astronomers spotted KIC 8462852, otherwise known as Tabby's Star. Tabby's Star appears to go very dim from time to time. No one can really explain why. One suggestion is that a Dyson Ring—a version of the sphere—is absorbing its light.

BEHIND THE THEORY

The British writer Herbert George "H.G." Wells wrote the most famous alien invasion story, *War of the Worlds*, in 1898. In the story, the invaders are Martians who arrive in three-legged fighting machines that can **vaporize** human defenders with an awesome heat ray. The Martians want to turn Earth into a new version of Mars, and they survive by drinking the blood of humans and other animals. In the end, the Martians are killed by infection from Earth's germs. In the story, humans survive—but live forever in fear of future attacks.

If so, the people of Tabby's Star could be in danger of a visit from unwelcome guests. Stars do not last forever. (Our sun only has 5 billion years to go.) When a civilization's star begins to die, it might look for another place to live. The best place to go will be to another civilization that already has a Dyson Sphere—like Tabby's Star—and take over. Once civilizations learn to travel anywhere in the galaxy, then the chance of an invasion by aliens increases. Perhaps we had better not look too hard for aliens—in case they decide to visit!

Is the dimming of Tabby's Star created by an artificial disk around it?

41

WILL ALIENS EVER ARRIVE?

In the middle of the twentieth century, the Italian physicist Enrico Fermi pointed out a **paradox**, or contradiction, in how we think about aliens. We know the chance that alien civilizations exist is high. We know the chance that some are advanced enough to travel across space is also high. However, we also know that no aliens have ever visited and there is no evidence of them. Fermi saw this contradiction—the Fermi Paradox—as proof that aliens do not exist.

Alpha Centauri, the nearest star after the sun, is four light-years away.

To reach the nearest stars now, the fastest-ever spacecraft, *Juno*, would have had to take off when the ancient Egyptians were building the pyramids.

The nearest stars to Earth are the Alpha Centauri group. The light from those stars takes four years to reach us. Any radio message we sent to Alpha Centauri would take eight years to get a reply. The fastest spacecraft ever built would reach Alpha Centauri in … 4,500 years! The Milky Way is 100,000 light-years across, so if aliens are on the way to us, they will be traveling for a long time yet.

Many scientists now believe that aliens are almost certainly out there. Some of them might be intelligent enough to be our friends (or enemies). However, we are all too far apart to ever find out. We are not alone—but we can never meet.

UNANSWERED

The scale of the galaxy and universe means that travel to the stars is difficult to comprehend. A city-sized starship could use solar sails to capture light pressure, which is a push given by the sun. Large sails could drive the starship to about one-tenth of the speed of light. However, it would take centuries to reach that speed. Even then, a voyage to an alien world could take many more lifetimes. No one who set off would ever arrive, but their descendants would. Want to come along?

1400 BC — Ancient Egyptians record the first sighting of an unidentified flying object.

1543 — Polish astronomer Nicolaus Copernicus places the sun rather than Earth at the center of the solar system.

1877 — Italian astronomer Giovanni Schiaparelli maps the surface of Mars. His map of the planet's "canals" starts a period of intense speculation about whether Mars is home to a civilization.

1894 — US businessman Percival Lowell opens an observatory near Flagstaff, Arizona, to look for life on Mars.

1898 — English writer H.G. Wells writes *War of the Worlds*, one of the most famous science-fiction stories about alien invasion.

1903 — The Russian Konstantin Tsiolkovsky suggests rocket travel to other planets. His colleague, Gavriil Tikhov, considers the conditions required for life on other planets, becoming the first astrobiologist.

1912 — US astronomer Vesto Slipher uses the Lowell Observatory to discover that other galaxies are moving away from Earth.

1935 — Romanian engineer Henri Coanda designs a flying saucer.

1936 — TV signals broadcasting the Berlin Olympics are the first radio signals to travel beyond Earth.

1947 — In the Roswell Incident, an alien spacecraft is rumored to have crash-landed in New Mexico and been covered up by US authorities.

1950 Nuclear scientist Enrico Fermi coins the Fermi Paradox. If the universe is full of intelligent civilizations, where are all the aliens?

1952 US scientist Stanley Miller performs an experiment to replicate the conditions for the creation of life on Earth.

1961 US scientist Frank Drake creates the Drake Equation to calculate the chances of intelligent life existing elsewhere in the universe.

1972 US UFO expert J. Allen Hynek publishes a system for classifying "close encounters" with aliens.

1974 Frank Drake and US scientist Carl Sagan broadcast the Arecibo Message into space.

1977 Carl Sagan includes disks bearing messages to aliens onboard the *Voyager* probes.

1984 The Search for Extraterrestrial Intelligence (SETI) begins scanning the universe for evidence of radio signals from aliens.

1992 Radio astronomers announce the first confirmed discovery of an exoplanet.

1996 Signs of microbial life are discovered inside a meteorite from Mars, ALH84001, discovered in Antarctica in 1984.

2012 The rover *Curiosity* lands on Mars to continue the search for evidence of life.

2024 The Extremely Large Telescope (ELT) is scheduled to go into service in Chile.

2025 The *Europa Clipper* is scheduled to fly to Jupiter's fourth moon to take samples of the ocean beneath its crust of ice.

GLOSSARY

acid rain rain formed of acidic liquids

aliens beings that originate in other worlds rather than Earth

atmosphere a ball of gases surrounding a planet

autopsy a medical examination of a body to find out the cause of death

bacteria microscopic living organisms that usually have a single cell

biochemistry the study of the chemicals and chemical reactions that support life

biologists scientists who study living things and life processes

black holes points of space where mass and gravity are so dense that not even light can escape

carbon a chemical element that is the basis for all life on Earth

cells the units that make up living things

civilization an advanced stage of human development and social organization

colony a settlement established by a group of people in another place

equation a mathematical formula to solve a particular problem

galaxy a group of millions or billions of stars held together by gravity

gravity a force that makes solid bodies attract one another

greenhouse effect the phenomenon in which gases trap heat from the sun in Earth's atmosphere

habitable zone the region around a star in which conditions may be able to support life

hoax a deliberate deception

hypothesis a possible explanation of something based on limited evidence

meteorite a piece of rock or metal that falls to Earth from space

microbes tiny, single-celled organisms

Milky Way Earth's galaxy

molecules joined groups of atoms

observatory a building that houses a telescope

paradox a statement that seems contradictory but may well be true

planet a celestial body orbiting a star

probes Spacecraft designed to visit other planets

radio the transmission of electromagnetic waves through space

radioactive powered by decaying atoms

reactive responding to conditions

science fiction stories based on scientific theories and advances

solar panels panels that absorb heat from the sun to use as energy

solar systems groups of planets orbiting the same star

solar wind an electrified current that radiates through space from the sun

species a related group of living things

vaporize to turn something solid into gas so that it disappears

BOOKS

Aguilar, David A. *Alien Worlds: Your Guide to Extraterrestrial Life*. National Geographic Children's Books, 2013.

Coddington, Andrew. *Aliens*. New York, NY: Cavendish Square Publishing, 2016.

Hawksett, David. *Extraterrestrials: Can You Find Them in the Universe?* New York, NY: PowerKids Press, 2018.

Kenney, Karen Latchana. *Exoplanets: Worlds Beyond Our Solar System*. Minneapolis, MN: Twenty First Century Books, 2017.

WEBSITES

Astrobiology **money.howstuffworks.com/astrobiologist.htm**
How Stuff Works explains what astrobiologists do.

Drake Equation **www.bbc.com/future/story/20120821-how-many-alien-worlds-exist**
This page from the BBC allows readers to figure out for themselves the chances of alien civilizations existing.

Life in Space **www.esa.int/esaKIDSen/SEMNOIWJD1E_LifeinSpace_0.html**
Pages for kids from the European Space Agency—use the menu on the right.

SETI **coolcosmos.ipac.caltech.edu/ask/248-What-is-the-SETI-project-**
A page from Cal Tech with a description of the SETI Project.

Publisher's note to educators and parents: Our editors have carefully reviewed these websites to ensure that they are suitable for students. Many websites change frequently, however, and we cannot guarantee that a site's future contents will continue to meet our high standards of quality and educational value. Be advised that students should be closely supervised whenever they access the Internet.

INDEX